still

growing

wildflowers

Copyright © 2020 Alisha Galbraith | Where She Grows

All rights reserved.

ISBN: 9781674064604

CONTENTS

the roots .... pg. 5

the weeds .... pg. 31

the rain .... pg. 91

the breaking .... pg. 121

still growing ....…......…..…....... pg. 175

Here's to you:

Don't ever let people use who you *used to be* as a weapon. Fun fact: people change. To anyone who is growing and feeling choked by the weeds: you are allowed to change. You are allowed to grow into someone new. Don't let anyone steal your sunshine or uproot you.

This book is for you. You're still growing wildflowers.

The roots.

still growing wildflowers

roots

trailing

down my skin

this is where

we begin.

where she grows

Riding on a bike

mint green

down a West Covina street

    --a memory

still growing wildflowers

Shots fired

Bullet hole to the chest

Numb yet you've never felt pain like this

Cover the wound with your fist and

Now you have two choices left

Heal

Or bleed to death

    —-*trigger warning*

where she grows

the sun is shining

I am just two doors away

playing in the sand on the west side of the house

I am only seven years old

I can see the road and

I am building moats around

mountains of sand

The older boys run a wheelbarrow

through the water

and around the house over and over

my brother and sister go for a ride a few times

and they're laughing

it looks fun

but I'm happy where I am

building moats around mountains of sand

still growing wildflowers

then

it's your turn

one boy says to me and it makes me feel scared

I say no

but everyone says it's so fun

so I climb in

alone

I'm bouncing and bumping as we go

around the house

East side this time

but not where I can see the road

he stops the ride

I'm about to climb out and he says

do you want to play a game

close your eyes

where she grows

I am only seven years old

I just wanted to build moats

around mountains of sand

The sun is shining

and

I am two doors away from home

    --I am not the only one

still growing wildflowers

tears won't stop falling

onto my parent's bed

word of god heavy under my hands

that still feel dirty

and I'm trying to understand if I am

still worthy to be loved

if this is my sin

what should I have done different

you come into the room and

I see the panic in your eyes

seeing me cry and you ask

what's wrong

where she grows

and I sob that

I'm just feeling the holy spirit

because I know the grownups at church cry and say it

and I don't know how to tell you

what happened that day

your eyes relax

relieved

as you hug me and tell me

you are glad for me

and I cry

    ---my first big lie

still growing wildflowers

The quiet girl

The shy girl

The dark haired

big brown eyed sad girl

no one ever asked why this girl

prefers to be alone

now you know.

where she grows

After that it was easy to spot them

The men who were good

And the ones who were not

Brick house on the left

My neighbor

Cigarette smoke

Voice like sandpaper and gravel

Usually drunk

But safe

At least for kids

Sometimes his girlfriend would call the police

But I knew he would never hurt me

like the boy with

the wheelbarrow

still growing wildflowers

White house on the right

My neighbor

We helped him rake leaves.

His wife would bake cookies.

He wore suspenders.

And he was safe.

The babysitter.

Same age as the boy with

the wheelbarrow

But safe.

where she grows

My dad's best friend

Liked flowers and cross stitch

Laughed and hugged me

And he was safe.

when I was eight my mother told me to never be

alone with a man

because you never know

what could happen.

But I did

And it was too late.

still growing wildflowers

The sun is shining. It usually is. You know those days when you lived for recess? This is one of those. Someone is playing tag and I start running. I'm not too fast but I can run longer than most of the boys. Running back and forth, back and forth and more join in. I think this is a game so I'm running back and forth, back and forth then bam. He's on top of me. Then another and another and another and there are fists and arms and I'm screaming for them to get off, they are heavy, I can't breathe and I don't know what's going on but I see my brother running to help me and he grabs a boy and throws him off, reaches for another and then I can't see anymore. I don't even know how it ends. But I know this panic. I've felt it before. Suddenly they are gone. I try to be tough and my little brother asks if I'm alright even though I'm pretty sure he's been punched in the eye and then he runs inside because he is late for class. I don't know how I get to my seat, but I do and then the principal calls me to the library. He's safe. I think my brother told someone what happened. That's why I'm here in the library now sitting at a table across from the boy who started it. Whatever "it" was. We have the same birthday. I wonder if he knows. He tells the safe man "we were just having fun" as I stare at my hands clenched on the table and tears dance on the rims of my eyelids, until they slip quietly down my cheeks. BAM the safe man slams his hands on the table and he yells "does she look like she's having fun?" He makes the boy look at me and I can't meet his eyes even though I want to so I can say I'm okay. You didn't break me. Instead I cry.

—third grade

still growing wildflowers

You deserved to feel safe

you should have been able to tell someone

without being afraid

you did not deserve this pain

I am here

I am sorry

We will get through this together

--what I wish I heard when I

told you the truth

where she grows

rough skin

trailing up your limbs

wearing your favorite summer color

bits of light shining down on us

ladybugs

climbing all over the place

in grandmother's arms

I am safe

    --my favorite tree

still growing wildflowers

she doesn't like to be touched

they laugh

and I laugh too

because what else am I supposed to do

when my abuse is the noose you use

to make a joke.

where she grows

careless hair

wearing yellow like I'm the sun

an uncomfortable smile that says

do I belong here

are we done

when can we leave

there isn't enough space

between you and me

    -- some things never change

still growing wildflowers

You can try and twist it a thousand different ways

but only one truth remains

love is not pain

    --stop defending him

        --stop defending them

where she grows

When you're too brown

but not brown enough

So mixed that

you don't know where you fit

kids calling names that they heard their parents say

you don't even know what they mean or why they're

saying it

when your skin color is the same

    --another type of memory

still growing wildflowers

I once met a wise brown man

wrinkled hands

who talked to himself sometimes

but he was kind to me

even if he wasn't kind to himself

one morning making coffee

I turn and he looks at me and asks

why are you so sad

who made you so sad

he saw the hurt I carried

even though it was buried so deep

I couldn't see it.

where she grows

it was the fight in her

that made her beautiful

it said

I will not be held prisoner by this pain

so she set it free.

still growing wildflowers

she was a bit like spring

wild as the wind and fickle as the weather

but her love ran deep as tree roots.

where she grows

I'm feeling better now. It's not so dark, not so foggy. It was probably all a dream. I'm feeling better now when the sun comes up instead of wishing it didn't come up at all. I'm feeling better now and that's all I can ask for.

still growing wildflowers

Hello beautiful,

I see you reaching for the sunshine.

-like a sunflower.

The weeds.

I forgive you. I forgave you a long time ago, but it doesn't erase the memories stored in my skin or the crushing weight in my ribs. Writing gives key to the cage and allows me to escape so just to be clear I understand that this is hard to hear, hard to read, but I hope you can see that these were the seeds you planted in me. It just turns out they were weeds.

where she grows

peace

that's all I wanted from you

well

actually

that isn't true

I wanted to know you

what you were like as a child

I know I got my wild side from somewhere

was it you

still growing wildflowers

I wanted to be the reason you smiled instead of

being the cause of your resentment

with a target on my back

I wanted what the others had with you

it's true

but now

peace

will do.

where she grows

are you afraid?

yes. but not for the reason you think.

I'm afraid I'll walk away and

you'll stop loving me.

    --letter to my parents

still growing wildflowers

Some mothers

do harm

words like knives

shots fired

from hands

meant to hold you

and keep you safe

    --laced with drugs and alcohol

where she grows

other mothers

do harm

words like knives

shots fired

from hands

meant to hold you

and keep you safe

    --completely sober

still growing wildflowers

your words the whip and

my body the cedar post

not giving in this time.

where she grows

the black sheep

--it's a skin I wear proudly now

still growing wildflowers

Call me a heathen

I'd rather be on fire

than pouring holy water

on others while they drown.

where she grows

Maybe this time

the bite won't leave a mark I say

as my flesh starts to decay

    your words like venom in my veins.

still growing wildflowers

You do not get to pick and choose

the parts of me that you love as

if you're picking petals from a flower

love me

        love me not

                love this

                        not that

throwing them down on the grass while I'm asking

        do you love me

                do you love me

                      do you love me yet

by the time you are done pulling at the core

there is nothing left for you to love anymore.

where she grows

The sound of a door

opening too quickly

never knowing

what version of you

is coming after it

    --a trigger

        The sound of a door

        slamming as you leave behind it

        not knowing

        if you were coming back this time

        --a relief

still growing wildflowers

selfish

selfish

selfish

the word my mother used to describe me most

so I learned to be quiet

my feelings are hurt

SELFISH

I disagree

SELFISH

This makes me happy

SELFISH

I don't believe

SELFISH

where she grows

and I learned to give in

with her *echoing* in my head

this isn't what I want

SELFISH

please wait

SELFISH

I'm not ready

SELFISH

No

SELFISH.

still growing wildflowers

I'm suffocating in this small space

Part of it is the fact that

We're in the front seat of the car

Part of it is

That you're on top of me

When I didn't ask you to be

And I already told you no

Your energy

Dark

where she grows

Rapacious

Greedy little fingers

Ransacking my body

and I can't move back and

I already told you no

This is what they warned you about

I do what I have to so I don't end up in a grave

Separate from my body

and wait.

still growing wildflowers

Where does love leave you

Crying on the bathroom floor

In an empty house you call home

feeling lonely, but not alone

wondering if you'll ever be enough

wondering if this will be the

last time

they leave

they cheat

they lie

they break you

where she grows

where oh where does love leave you

begging for forgiveness though there is nothing to be

forgiven but you know if you didn't you may as well

tie your own noose

where does love leave you, my dear

if this is you

love wasn't ever there.

still growing wildflowers

I pray

that I am not too proud to say

I am so sorry

I made a mistake

you were right

I love you all the way.

where she grows

you are the man

I thought I'd never lose

the one I thought I'd never

have to prove myself to

but the more I changed

the more I could see

you only loved your version

of me.

still growing wildflowers

I didn't ask for your advice

    I asked for your love

        Now I know it was too much.

where she grows

Can you smell the fear on my skin

like I haven't showered in days?

    --easy prey

still growing wildflowers

I go through my days quietly

trying not to make waves

but one whisper creates ripples in the sleeping sea

don't make a sound I say

too late

it's awake

    --tsunami

where she grows

what color do you bleed

you asked as you cut me down again

in the end you'd see

you'd have to rip me out from the roots

    --still growing wildflowers

still growing wildflowers

the abuse never should have happened

especially at the hands of the one who grew you

but because they raised you

they expect you to bury your bones

but how can you heal a wound

if you never take out the thorns

when they throw you into the bush

then look at the blood on your arms and say

I don't know where it came from

    clean it up.

where she grows

You

could have ended the cycle of

broken mother-daughter relationships but

You

chose power over love

You

cannot put this on me

because I chose

You

time after time

and it was never enough for

You

and in the end

I chose love for

Me.

still growing wildflowers

You and I are under the same sky

but the view is different from here

    --perspective

where she grows

At night

when you put them to sleep

and tell them tall tales of

the wayward black sheep

who was bitter and bad

but why, oh why

you just don't understand

do you also describe

how you tried

to skin me alive

with your teeth?

still growing wildflowers

I hang on to broken things in hope of fixing them.

But let's be honest,

some things weren't meant to be fixed.

This is one of those things.

where she grows

It takes two

To fall apart

And come together again

But you kept an ocean between us

Without a lighthouse on the shore and

I slipped on the rocks trying to get to your door

Left my blood in the water

While the salt kissed my wounds

It takes two

And I am done

Chasing you.

still growing wildflowers

I spend so many nights wondering

if you'd ever defend me

defend us

and then you told me that I was the cause

of all your worst fights

why would I stay?

    --eighteen

where she grows

I was the hunted

easy prey

licking my wounds each time I escaped

and let you come back to take what was left

now

I am the huntress

try and take what is left

arrows up, love

here I come

    --I was born an archer

still growing wildflowers

Of course you tried

Of course there were good times

But for how long

And why

What do you want in return

        -skeptic

where she grows

I have learned that

it is a privilege to be in my life

not a daily battle where we have to pick sides

or force others to decide

who they love more

I used to care

but not anymore.

still growing wildflowers

I spent years picking myself apart

trying to find the reason why

but my fingers came up empty every time

where she grows

Stop digging for dead flowers.

still growing wildflowers

I learned a lot from you

But I never learned how to love me

Loving you

Made me feel small

Leaving you

Set me free.

where she grows

I don't want to make war anymore

and I won't be held hostage to your love

I am done mending fences

when you have no remorse

for setting fires in my home while I'm

trying to hold back the burning with my hands

how much gasoline

do you have left for me

white flag is up

I concede.

still growing wildflowers

what was it like to bring my life into the world

was my soul too much for you to handle

so you cut me down

to watch my petals fall at your feet

or did I take so much of you

that you could never forgive me

    --a question to my mother

where she grows

you called me selfish so many times it was like a

second name

I still turn my head when I hear someone say it

criticizing every part of me

scrutinizing my tendencies

you can't wear that

don't talk that way

while you

couldn't contain your rage

your hand striking like a snake

the target

my face

still growing wildflowers

and once was enough to know that this was not love

no matter how many times you lied through your

teeth telling me *God told me you were special*

like it mattered to me when you couldn't even say it

without clenching your teeth

    --the way you loved me

where she grows

the noble one

protected by god

full of grace and glory

keeper of the keys

you gave me the name of a queen

      did you forget?

still growing wildflowers

Her spirit was fire just like mine and she was the most loving, caring, bossy big sister you could ask for. I never resented being second-born, or in your eyes, second best, because I knew I wasn't, our paths were just different. I wish you could have seen it too. My flame was just as bright, just as strong, it was just a different hue. And it took me so long to forgive myself for letting you down as gently as you can break a heart and I'm sorry again, for doing it now.

where she grows

Just because our tragedies are not the same does not mean I don't feel pain. I know how hearts bleed.

still growing wildflowers

I still remember the things you said about me when you thought I couldn't hear. I know I wasn't perfect, but neither were you. You called me names, mine were silenced with a hand then buried in my body escaping through the back door in the middle of the night into the arms of someone with kinder hands.

where she grows

we're all just walking around to different places with mirrors on our faces and you hated your reflection so deeply that you broke mine to pieces.

still growing wildflowers

I could have done better

I could have tried harder

I could have given you more

But then

There would be nothing left

Of me.

where she grows

The air finally escapes my lungs

I've been holding my breath for far too long

Watching you walk on the daisies I left at your door

While you asked for more and

I grew what I could but it was

Never enough

    Not enough

        Enough

I've been holding my breath for far too long and the air finally escapes my lungs as I'm picking up the daisies I left at your door

        Enough

        Enough

I am enough

still growing wildflowers

I was blind and you spit at my feet and the dust turned to mud so I picked it up and put it on my eyes and now I can see you clearly.

    --ravening wolves

where she grows

Today

I forgive you

I forgive you for hating me

I forgive you for the blame

I forgive you

For every moment you made me wonder

if I was worth the air I breathed

I forgive you

for all of the apologies I never got

never heard but damn sure deserved

still growing wildflowers

I forgive you for the names

I forgive you for ignoring my pain with a smile on

your face like it

made it okay

Today

I forgive you

if only for me.

where she grows

sometimes the strongest storms

make the fiercest sunsets.

still growing wildflowers

this is how I want to be treated

this is how I don't want to be treated

take it or leave it

    —boundaries

where she grows

Dear boy,

here are some things I want you to remember:

There is strength in being soft

to look at someone and

Feel what they're feeling

And offer your arms as a refuge

You can be both gentle and wild

Tears do not mean you are weak

Everyone deserves kindness including your Self

Be strong in your truth

Share your light with those who have none

Keep your curiosity and wonder

Love even the smallest creatures

Be good to the earth

And even better to people.

still growing wildflowers

This is not a day wasted

holding you

wiping your tears

all of my best days

are with you

this is not a day wasted

throwing rocks in the water

watching ripples kiss the shore

all of my best days

are with you

    --raising my own

where she grows

my body is made of mountains, hills, and valleys that created and carried life, yet you'd like me to hide until I'm a little less broken and dirty. but I'm still growing wildflowers on this body made of mountains, hills, and valleys. I created and carried life. I will not hide.

still growing wildflowers

Like carrying the whole universe inside me

        --what it was like bringing your life
        into the world

        this is the difference

where she grows

loving you is the easiest thing

    when they put you on my chest

    I felt like my soul left my body

    and I was holding the stars in my arms

        --the day you were born

still growing wildflowers

A few things I hope you know:

my love is not something you have to earn.

it just is.

you can come to me for anything.

your feelings matter.

I trust you.

I believe you.

I am proud of you.

all of my best days are with you.

the rain.

still growing wildflowers

are you ready

they cried as they

held back the sky

and the light danced

in waves

here comes the rain.

where she grows

sometimes it doesn't matter

how hard you pray

pain is going to happen to you anyway

    And no one escapes death.

        Not even the best.

still growing wildflowers

I saw the bruises

shaped like fingers on your arms

I even asked about them

but I misread the fear in your eyes

for anger when you whispered

DON'T

both a warning and a plea

I am so sorry

that I never said anything more

now I always wonder

what happened behind the doors

of the place you called home.

530

It's too early for phone calls

But I wake up to my phone buzzing

Then it stops

Moments later

Another call

Because something isn't right

Your sister is in the hospital

The baby is alright but

She has bleeding

On her brain

And it does not look good

I will let you know more

When I know more

still growing wildflowers

535

Making a phone call

To a bishop's home

Strangers

Apologizing because

I know it's early but

My sister is in the hospital

And my mother requested you come

Because my father

Is working

Out of the country

I'm so sorry for

The trouble

where she grows

600

Waiting

Hoping

But it's like I already know

                                                                                     700

                                                           Phone call

                                                              Calmly

                                        Please call your siblings

                                        Tell them if they'd like

                                                      To say goodbye

                                        They should come now

still growing wildflowers

715

Calling

Slow breathing

Keep emotions in line

Hi

Mom said we can come

Say goodbye

Do you need a ride?

Okay

Be sure to eat something

I know you don't feel like it

where she grows

But it will help keep you

From going into shock

Even just a piece of bread

I'll see you there

I love you.

                                                Repeat.

                                                Repeat.

                                                Repeat.

                                             I choke on

                                             The last call

                                           My tears won't

                                              Stop falling.

                                    * timeline of the reaper

still growing wildflowers

Sunset light fading

Can you wish on a flower

Hold my breath and wait.

where she grows

I remember your last sunset

as you were lying in the room

they moved quietly in whispers giving you gifts

you'd never use

as they prepared you for death saying

thank you

thank you

thank you

I moved down the hall

the room was far too crowded

to hear you at all anyway

still growing wildflowers

and though it was such a relief

to know that you'd be free

I stood there

holding back the rain

and watched the pink sky fade

knowing this was your last sunset

with me.

where she grows

tick

tock

tick

tock

every minute

every second

heads bow

pray

they say

still growing wildflowers

tick tock

tick tock

the clock is screaming now

wake up

wake *up*

can you hear how death is calling

tick

tock

tick

tock

time

stops.

where she grows

I remember it like yesterday

blue skies and no rain

there's a beating in my chest

hollow heart that sounds like regret

all the things I should have done

should have said

left for dead

like the flowers by your bed

now

the flowers still bloom without you

and they always remind me of you.

still growing wildflowers

I'll send you my love on butterfly wings.

where she grows

the earth mourns the ones we've lost

quivers and shakes and breaks like we do

she turns our screams into sunsets

our secrets to stars with the moon to hold your

sorrow wherever you are

she turns our tears into flowers

grown through the dirt

and though the world keeps on turning

she feels your hurt.

still growing wildflowers

People ask why I take so many photos of insignificant things. It's because one day I woke up to a phone call telling me our sister was in the hospital. Within a few days she was suddenly memories and old photographs. Someone whose name we without realizing started whispering and saying less. When people ask why I take so many photos, it's so I don't forget.

where she grows

and for everyone else today is a normal day

--the anniversary of a death

still growing wildflowers

It's hard for me to imagine your body under ground

I know how things decay so

I imagine flowers growing from your eyes

and vines wrapping your bones because

I know

how things decay.

where she grows

when I die

make me a tree

take my ashes

bury me

take my ashes

over the plains

through the meadows

to the mountain rain

still growing wildflowers

when I die

make me a tree

take my ashes

bury me

in the place

where the wildflowers grow

as the wind whispers like sunlight

through my soul

when I die

make me a tree

take my ashes

bury me.

where she grows

I imagine you're in the stars

in the sunset and

all across the sea

even though you're gone

I imagine you're here with me.

                    still growing wildflowers

pulling in air

like I'm picking up boulders

and it's exhausting

hold steady

inhale

exhale

why is breathing so heavy?

where she grows

Living

but death has its hold on me

I think of you every day.

still growing wildflowers

now death is like a leaky sink

asking me

if today was the last day you breathed

did you do enough

love enough

make enough memories to last their lifetime

a slow drip

on the life I'm trying to live.

where she grows

this grief

these tears

are sacred

I am honored to have loved someone so much

it still moves me

these tears

this grief

are sacred

I am honored to have been loved by you so much

I still feel it.

    --the stars between us

still growing wildflowers

And the moon will hold your secrets

the stars will catch your tears

the night will rock you softly

so go on, cry, my dear.

where she grows

I watched you

floating from plant to plant and

I wondered what you were doing

it looked like a struggle

almost like it was hard to breathe

wings lifting and

you didn't fly away from me

when I got close to see that you

were laying eggs on three-inch high milkweed

then I realized

you were dying

and my heart dropped out of my chest

because you were giving your last breath

for your child.

    --just like she did

still growing wildflowers

I am in the stars

and the stars are in me

so when you reach out to touch the sky

I'll feel you in my wings.

the breaking.

still growing wildflowers

you want the truth

here it is

they say the truth

will set you free

but sometimes first

      it takes everything.

where she grows

yes

I choked on the word

eyes wide

mouth dry

screaming inside

someone please save me

this isn't what I want

but it's what every girl wants

you should be so lucky

he's such a good man

but don't you see

it was over before it began

still growing wildflowers

eyes wide

mouth dry

Staring down at my

white dress

breathless

thinking

oh dear god

I take it back.

where she grows

When I finally have the courage to say

no

I'm not happy

I don't love you that way

it seems the only thing that matters

is filling your bed

instead of listening to what

I actually said

I didn't need you.

I chose you

and day after day

you didn't give me a reason to stay.

still growing wildflowers

Leave.

–things I'd do if I was brave

where she grows

The roots of your indifference

run under my skin like veins

pathways

and I forget who I am because I can't stop hearing

what you never said

    --apathy

still growing wildflowers

I told you once

I thought I wasn't clear

Told you twice

Thought maybe you didn't hear

I told you again and again and

Yet again and finally I realized

You heard me

You just didn't care

    --deaf ears

where she grows

it feels like a lifetime of stumbling

through the dark

wondering what will break the fall

    --the space between us

still growing wildflowers

I knew

but I didn't know how to undo what was done

just keep moving forward

one day at a time

they say you're doing what's right

the first year is the hardest

get through that and you can get through anything

six years later

I'm still swimming

and sinking quickly

    --drowning

where she grows

Be careful of the company you keep

sometimes the wolves look like sheep.

still growing wildflowers

trust

it's a word I don't understand

trust is built on the idea that someone

some day will save you

honey

I can't even trust myself

let alone anyone else.

We all carry different pain; what one person struggles with you could never imagine feeling that way. Even within loving partnerships and healthy friendships, we fight our own demons, alone. And most of us never dare share them for fear of being labeled as ungrateful, selfish, bad, troubled, wrong, or all of the above. It's hard enough to open up so instead of throwing stones, just love.

still growing wildflowers

I'm trying to be

more of me

and less of you

    --changing is good for people too

where she grows

I'm afraid to love anything too much

but only because you try

and make me feel guilty

for not loving you enough.

still growing wildflowers

Just because you don't see me cry

doesn't mean I'm happy

Not every storm brings rain.

people say live a life you love don't you dare spend one more minute living a life that doesn't bring you joy. and it seems so simple to let go, to be free when you're living a life you never thought you'd be. but it's hard to leave the ones you call family.

still growing wildflowers

We're ruled by fear;

fear of letting go

fear of choosing the wrong one

fear of loving too much

and my greatest fear is being afraid

to step into the unknown on my own

my greatest fear

is that I won't miss you when I go.

where she grows

there are lights

and stars in the sky

laughter and smiles and chatter

so much chatter that you can't hear

the shatter

    --lonely but not alone

still growing wildflowers

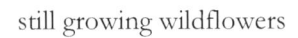

Please understand that I am not perfect. It is easier to show the scars we got from someone else than to show the ones we inflicted ourselves.

where she grows

he breathed life into me

and he didn't even touch me

It never should have happened

yet

it did and

    I'm sorry

seems like a shallow fix

for a wound so deep

I understand if you can never forgive me.

still growing wildflowers

I have flowers to tend

but I'm still here in bed and

I know in my head

that I have flowers to tend

they're pulling at the covers

and I'm screaming in my head

to get up get up get up

you have flowers to tend

but I'm still here in bed.

where she grows

she felt like rain

falling

falling

falling

..

still growing wildflowers

the world was on fire

everything I knew up in flames and I watched it burn

knowing I was the one who lit the match

but this

was not my intent

As the flowers turned to ash

and the sky became black

my cries for help fell on the ears of those who cried

you made your bed now lie

in it

as they fanned the flames

grasping at my feet

my blood finally quenching the thirst

ashes to ashes

dust to dust.

where she grows

And I'm lying in the sunlight

chest heavy

gasping for rays like they'll fill my chest with light

hands

clutching the grass

willing them to grow roots

and sprout flowers

from my lungs.

still growing wildflowers

the sky is on fire

but it seems that's nothing new

walking through the streets as embers fall

covered in soot

trying to brush away the ash to blend in

and all it does is stick to my skin.

where she grows

It's quiet now

the flames don't burn as bright and

I can feel the wind on my skin now

don't breathe too loud

checking for safety beneath singed brows

Alive

In one piece

but not unscathed

thank god for these roots.

still growing wildflowers

here's the thing about wildflowers

they take root wherever they are

grow strong through the wind, rain, pain, sunshine

blue skies and starless nights

they dance, even when it seems there is nothing

worth dancing for

they bloom

with or without you.

I have let you stay for far too long— your name your words taking up space in my body where you don't belong anymore. I have let you stay day after day, still growing wildflowers in the spaces where you dug out my flesh to bones. I have let you stay for far too long. But not anymore.

still growing wildflowers

I am a constant contradiction

reaching for peace

trying to tame the beast in my mind

the one that is unkind

telling me that I've done it all wrong

you don't deserve love

you should be happy here

because even this

is more than you deserve

    --you sound like my mother

where she grows

stop setting fires in your mind from the
matches others left for you to find.

TO THE GOD I ONCE KNEW

I don't like confrontation and I've been told to never question your will, but I've grown from an obedient child into a woman who is wild and challenges what I've been taught to believe.

I've done what you would have me do Instead of being true to myself. I moved to a place I can't stand, never could, said I would never get married, but I did that too because it's what You wanted. I got married out of obligation not of love or fascination trying to convince myself this is right, this is good, it's what God would have me do and he will fill up the space where, "I feel nothing for you."

I've been met with silence. Unanswered cries and they say, "all in His time". But I'm tired of waiting, hoping something will change before it's too late.

She was 28 when she died, and I thought 'maybe this is my sign' because just the week before I told her 'I can't do this anymore'. Then she was gone.

Is it my fault?

I shouldn't have cried I should have lied and said that I was happy just like I'd been doing since the day I got married. They tell me I'm so lucky, so blessed to be in this "mess" so I buried my feelings just like they buried my sister.

I miss her.

No amount of tears, cries, or lies to change my mind have been heard. I pray, please Your will, not mine. I'm tired of choking on please God why

why

why

why

why don't I feel it

why is she gone

why aren't you listening

this isn't what I want

please

still growing wildflowers

God please

just change my heart

silence

guilt

regret

now anger and yet I'm still holding on out of fear because I was taught your love is earned. Do what I say, and you'll be okay, so I gave up what I wanted most to please you:

I gave up me.

Finally, courage to break out and say this isn't what I'm about only to be met with pity and she doesn't really mean it she's gone through this before with warnings to be careful that I'm on a slippery slope but this is the first time in years that I have felt any hope. Tell me again that what I'm doing is a sin, that I must not care about my children because if I did, I wouldn't do *this*.

They don't know how many times I wish it was me to go, not her, because this is a life she wanted a life she deserved. I wonder if they know how many times I've gone to sleep wishing that you'd take my soul to keep, how many times I've given in and said I love you with my skin while I held back the tears and wished I wasn't in it.

But *his* will not mine.

I wonder if they know how many times I've agonized over the right thing to do how many times I've asked *you.*

but they say I lack faith

I'm not trying enough

all in *His* time

it's *fine.*

…

but I'd like to move on, it's not you, it's me; because what's the point if you're not listening?

To the god I once knew: I've changed

Have you?

where she grows

Happiness is subjective and

it's based on perspective and

cultural opinion and

if there's one thing religion taught me

is that judgment begins the moment

you push your idea of

happiness on someone else.

I will not force you to understand mine.

still growing wildflowers

what happened to you

they ask me

like I've gotten sick with the flu

and they might catch it too

and when I tell them

I just woke up one day

they look at me and say

I'll pray

for you.

    --heathen

where she grows

No

Please don't pray for me

pray for you

that you'll accept and love me

no matter what I choose

    --my life, not yours

still growing wildflowers

I get so tired of trying to explain my heart

to those who cannot feel their own.

Please allow yourself to grow. let yourself see another perspective. listen. cry. love. I mean, really love. Your way is not the only way life is done. Please allow people to change without trying to make them feel like they need saving when it is you who is uncomfortable with the changing.

still growing wildflowers

how does it taste

the fire coming from your lips

pull the trigger in the name of the holy one

spit smoke

lock and load

how long have you been keeping score

one shot

two shots

three shots

more

are you done?

where she grows

the day will come when you realize

the things you condemned in me

were the things you despised in you

    --this is judgment day

still growing wildflowers

and when they say

you've changed

you tell them

no

I have always been this way

it is you

who tried to keep me in a cage.

where she grows

This drink is bitter

and it suits me

the taste shocking me back into the present

I spend too long trapped in daydreams

it's hard to swim back up to reality

I only have so much breath left in my lungs

this drink is bitter

and it suits me

    --drinking coffee at noon

still growing wildflowers

I am not afraid to navigate these waters alone

ever moving

flowing

wild

etching its way through the earth

I am not afraid to navigate these waters alone

I am afraid

of drowning in the boat you put me in.

where she grows

When an infant is crying

Saying, "help me, please"

We respond quickly

Get the baby what it needs;

Food

Sleep

A hug

A kiss

As children we ask easily;

"Help me, please"

But we don't get help as quickly as the infant

And there are times when we are met with

"Just a minute"

"Hold on, I'm busy"

"It can wait".

In adolescence our "help me, please"

is again met less quickly,

still growing wildflowers

Has us wondering if people are listening

So we learn to stop asking for help by the time we

transition into adulthood

Suddenly it becomes weak

To say

"Help me, please"

We go days and weeks and months and years

Without asking for help

And when we finally have the courage

To speak up and say,

"Help me, please, I can't live this way anymore"

We're met with

"Just a minute"

"Hold on, I'm busy"

"It can wait."

where she grows

It cannot wait.

By the time we have spoken up we are at the end of our rope.

"Help me, please" looks like

Someone not answering their texts

Disinterest in things they used to love

Someone asking for a hug

To go to the movies

To go for a walk

To be loved unconditionally

For the freedom to change

still growing wildflowers

"Help me, please" looks like

A smile we wish we were given

Success that keeps hurt hidden

Normal to you days and nights

"I don't have the energy to fight"

And if there's one thing We wish you knew;

"Help, please" looks like me.

And it looks like you.

where she grows

I know today is tough and

that it's hard to see the light and

that breathing isn't easy but please

keep fighting

it will be alright.

still growing wildflowers

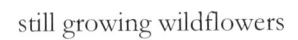

And if flowers can grow through cracks in the sidewalk then you can get through this.

where she grows

Only you can heal me

she said to the pieces shattered on the floor

only you

as she moved the shards of glass

    blood on her hands

    putting it back together again

seven years bad luck they say when a mirror breaks

but this is the beginning of healing.

still growing wildflowers

Laying in the grass

Looking up at the trees

Remembering when I used to climb

Through the leaves

That sound like a river in the wind and

Suddenly

It stops

And I hear her say

When did You

stop being brave?

still growing.

still growing wildflowers

sunlight

dances on my skin

like fingertips

feet

rooting in the earth as she whispers

you are ready

even though it hurts

    --blooming

where she grows

sometimes it's okay

to bury your pain

after you've let it sit

in the rain

this is how

wildflowers are made.

still growing wildflowers

please share your battle scars. tell us how you chased away demons with nothing but bones and smoke. let the others know that you live even after you bleed.

    --healers

where she grows

she's' not lost she is free

and this is her rising

don't you see her wings?

    --you only know half the story

still growing wildflowers

I've been told all the things I should love about me that I don't actually know what *I* love about me. It's all just a picture we paint of ourselves, of each other, what we wish others would see, but is that really me? I'm learning to love me as *I am* not as you want me to be.

this is healing.

where she grows

things I stopped apologizing for:

	changing

still growing wildflowers

the view from here is different now because we don't see eye to eye and I am no longer willing to apologize for making you uncomfortable.

where she grows

Thunderstorm

Dripping rain. Fierce wind.

Sigh of relief.

    --no longer screaming

still growing wildflowers

It's dark

but I am not afraid

From corner of my eye a buck darts

through the trees

I step away from my safe place

Down

Down

Down the steps

Into the grass

Bare feet

where she grows

I walk

And walk

And walk

The sky turning pink

I come to a tree

With butterflies for leaves

Orange wings that take flight when I exhale

But one floats gently into my outstretched hand

Clear wings like glass

I am free.

still growing wildflowers

What if we saw each other as galaxies and stars

instead of broken and scarred?

where she grows

I used to love you. And my greatest fear was losing you and when it happened, I broke -- pain seeping through the pores in my skin. Would I ever, ever, ever come back together again? I used to love you so much I couldn't breathe when you left me and now, I see that *you* were not worthy of *me*. The day you left was the day you set me free. Thank you.

still growing wildflowers

you are the sun

but you can only warm a body

when it steps into the light

where she grows

Have you ever watched a butterfly emerge from her skin? She's enclosed in a shell; soft at first, and then it becomes hard, a protection against those that could hurt her--a shield to keep herself safe.

In this space she literally dissolves, falls apart, collapsed lungs, broken heart, hides her face. You wouldn't even recognize her anymore. And it's dark. So dark

She wonders if she's even breathing, if she's even worth seeing. But there in the dark is the smallest point of light. Even in the darkest black She was made to rise.

She wakes from her sleep, takes the chaos turned heartbeat, suddenly everything is clear. And those watching--they become still. Waiting.

She can't stay safe. She is breaking, as her seams start to burst there may be some hurt but this is her revolution and she's stronger than you think.

Finally, they can see what she was always meant to be. Some stand in awe, others are afraid, but she is a butterfly, she wasn't meant to be tamed. Softly she goes, ever silent, ever kind. Knowing when you change there are some you'll leave behind.

Have you ever watched a butterfly emerge from her skin? Darling, you are so much more than the box they put you in.

…

Being seen, heard, held, and honored for who you are in this exact moment is some of the most healing medicine on the planet. So, in case no one has told you today: I honor where you are and what you're feeling whether that be anger, regret, loneliness, guilt, shame or [insert what you're feeling here]. Sending you love.

Feeling is the alchemy of healing

still growing wildflowers

Finally, in your arms I can breathe.

I have not felt safe in so long.

where she grows

the universe

the stars

all that you are

    --limitless

still growing wildflowers

Mirror, mirror on the wall

looking at this form

flowers and scars

ending the war now

I love and accept myself

fully

I choose who to be

breathe

Mirror, mirror on the wall

looking into the soul

hearing the waves and the stories she holds

and now

I love and accept myself

I am whole

where she grows

Mirror, mirror on the wall

I see me

stars

moonlight

galaxies

this is what it means to be

perfect

you see

perfection

    is

        not what you think.

I'm in that weird healing space where you don't feel bad anymore, but you don't yet feel good. I'm in that weird healing space where you feel hollow...like you're standing in front of a path with multiple directions to choose from but you're unsure of moving forward because where you are feels safe, but you can't go back the way you came, and you're not sure which way you want to move anyway.

where she grows

in the morning she sighs and

in a single breath comes alive

all the rivers, lakes, and seas

mountains, deserts, and trees,

this good earth keeps giving to me.

still growing wildflowers

Please remember:

How you love yourself is how YOU love yourself.

You cannot teach everyone to love you well.

Do you like you?

Then that's enough.

where she grows

I spent so much of my life wanting to blend in

wondering if I could be a lighter shade on the canvas

would it be different

I used to wish I could change the color of my skin

my eyes

my hair

down to the color of my

brown

lips

and now

I love the color so much

that I never want to cover it up.

still growing wildflowers

He's five years old now and he's looking at my hands

while we're waiting in line and he asks

why are your hands a different color than mine

And I tell him that people

come from many different places

with all sorts of shades and colors and faces and

mine come from islands

where people are the color of chestnuts

and sweet coffee but

I also come from people

who are the color of ginger root and sand

and from people who are the color of

mushrooms, and cream and

they're all beautiful and together

they made me.

where she grows

he's seven now and

old enough to notice how

some people treat me differently

and I have to explain

racism

and how it still happens today.

--2019

still growing wildflowers

we are so much more

than skin and bones

I am not my body

I am my soul.

where she grows

I do not fear losing the light

The sun always comes back to me.

still growing wildflowers

I have not felt this alive in a long time.

This is how I know I'm healing.

    --dancing in the kitchen

where she grows

You know when the days are so good you can't

sleep?

maybe it's me

maybe it's the moon

maybe it's all this time I've spent with you.

still growing wildflowers

hello

good morning

I hope you see beauty today

even if it's hard to find

I hope you see

all of the light in you.

where she grows

I hope you always feel beautiful

I hope you always feel enough

I hope you always feel strong

and when you don't

I hope you remember

That you are

    still

        worth

            loving

                --note to self

still growing wildflowers

Things that make me feel free

sunshine

mountain air

ocean waves

messy hair

wildflowers

stormy skies

butterflies

    and yellow

..

where she grows

Instead of thinking you'll be happier somewhere else doing the next thing remind yourself that happiness is here underneath your feet

still growing wildflowers

Think of your healing as a seed; you're pushed into the dirt and everything is dark for a while. Some days you feel like you're literally drowning, then you start to soften up. The soil around you starts to warm, you feel the sun and start to break out of your shell, pushing a little further each day, even when it rains and hurts like hell. You keep growing through the weeds and the wind. And one day, you bloom. Not everyone will notice. Not everyone will care and there will be others who don't even like you. But the thing is, you didn't bloom for them. You bloomed for you.

where she grows

Confession: when I first saw a monarch, I thought they were too loud. Too bold, too big, too colorful, too bright, too orange, too flighty. And I'm sitting here realizing that I didn't like them because they were everything I was taught to dislike about myself. Too loud. Too bright. Too colorful. Too careless. Too bold. You can't wear that, don't talk like that, why can't you be like this, no, no, no.

Last year was my chrysalis. I was butterfly soup. But have you ever watched a butterfly emerge from her skin?

It's damn pretty.

So be too loud. Be too bright. Love too much. Because who you are is enough.

still growing wildflowers

Thank you

May your home be filled with wildflowers

and your heart filled with love.

    --a blessing from me to you

About the author

My name is Alisha.

I've never met a sunflower I didn't like.

Tree hugger.
Earth lover.
Wild mother.

That's how I would describe myself. I'm a kinda hippie, kinda witchy, sort of spiritual lifestyle-blogger at Where She Grows.

Sagittarius sun. Aries moon.
Pretty average human.

☮

Manufactured by Amazon.ca
Bolton, ON